Pieces Of Me

A collection of poetry and streams of consciousness

Rachel Louise Finn

Trigger Warning.

This book touches upon some very triggering themes, including;

self harm
suicide
eating disorders
depression
abuse
bullying
murder
and more.

Please look after yourself and practice self care if you are affected by any of these things.

preface

✤ Pieces Of Me is a life in poetry and streams of consciousness.

It chronicles a mind trying to piece itself together and a past trying to connect with the present.

In these pages are the rhymes and ramblings of a little girl lost, who spilled words onto paper to keep herself going.

She learned once again to bleed poetry out of her veins instead of cutting herself open.

It's a journey of a girl finding pieces of herself that she lost, pulling herself from the ashes, drowning in an ocean, discovering the world and herself, and *surviving, surviving, surviving.*

Pieces Of Me chronicles many journeys of one life, scrambled together to create a mess of words.

Places. People. Events. Feelings. Memories.

These are the pieces of me.

Maybe, somewhere in here, you'll be able to find a piece of you too.

Once upon a time, there was a little girl. Trapped in her tower, she stared out of the window and over the surrounding ocean, longingly watching the waves crash upon the shore.

Every day the little girl wished that she could be out there, dancing in the waves, singing with the gulls.

She dreamed her life away, locked in her room by the wicked witch. She felt uncomfortable in her body. She was unsteady on her feet.

All she could think about were those waves. The warm salty water. The shore, beautiful and adorned with shells and sparkling sea glass. The creatures that swam near the ocean floor. The colours and the wonders. So much more than this dreary world she was stuck in.

One day, the little girl planned to escape. She took a spoon from her breakfast tray - the only cutlery she was allowed as it was deemed the safest - and tirelessly worked away at the lock on the small window of her tower. Her heart was hammering away in her chest, threatening to burst out of her.

It took hours, hours, and hours. Her fingers worked and worked, skin splitting, agony threatening to overtake her.. but the little girl refused to give in. She couldn't stop. She just couldn't… *click!*

In the same second, she heard footsteps on the winding staircase that led up to her tower room. Each step echoing menacingly through the whole building. Frantic, she threw the now bent spoon to the floor and pulled with all the strength left in her poor, bloody fingers, shoving the window up, up, up…

The door flung open. The little girl turned. Staring back at her with wild eyes was the wicked witch, who let out a piercing shriek and suddenly moved, coming straight for her across the room.

Without a second thought, the little girl pulled herself up and over; throwing herself out of the window. Down, down, down, down… melting into sea foam the second she hit the water, while the witch shrieked after her in fury. Though she didn't hear a thing.

six word story: **Under the waves there is peace.**

Breathe.

It is all going to be fine.

Breathe.

Take this shit one day at a time.

Nostalgia

Nostalgia can hit you like a ton of bricks
Weighing you down from the very first hit.
Takes you back down some long winding roads
Romanticise the things you saw back then as heavy burning loads.

Truth is, your mind plays tricks on you,
Fools you into missing what you already outgrew.
Photographs can't capture the whole picture,
Pulls out the good parts and just hits you with it.

Take it with a grain of salt,
Don't let it make you halt
All the progress you have made.
The past is somewhere you cannot stay.

Spring flowers
brought up by the rain
Have me feeling
like a child again

Split

The fragmented child
Forlorn and wild.
The splintered soul
Will she ever be whole?

The fragmented girl
A fern that's unfurled.
Her splintered parts.
They tore her apart.

Still a girl living in high school hallways
Doesn't matter how many years pass
The feelings just never go away.

- *Trapped in bubbles of time #1*

Petals

All the innocence I ever had,
Was ripped from me
Piece by piece
Like petals ripped one by one from a flower.

*He loves me **not**.*

Rebel child
With nothing left to rebel against

Rebel girl
No use for all the fire you have left

- *You always burned too bright for any of them*

Barely a rhyme left in my head
Whatever poetry I used to have, it's dead

Barely a story left in my head.
Whatever words used to live in me are dead.

Barely a creative spark left in my mind
The writer who used to live in me is difficult to find.

Barely a word left in my mind
Who knew that the world was so unkind.

- *They took away my spark.*

I am locked away inside my own head
Trapped in a sphere of the past.
Trying to forget the words they said,
But these memories will always last.

I can't scream
Or nobody hears.

I can't get out
Trapped by my fears.

help

h e l p

HELP

From my tower

I scream,
        "save yourself".

In dreams,
        shadows of my past.

Shadows on the wall,
        watch me from the depths..

Monsters down the hall,
        the reason that I haven't slept.

Silence.
Keep your mouth *shut*.
Don't say a ~~word~~.

It's safer that way.

- *what they taught a child*

Fantasies

Drive the blade into your skull
Like all the nights I dreamed about.
Blood spilling onto the bedroom floor
As I stab and slash and scream and shout.

You never had to be so cruel
With the things that you said.
And now with hate, my heart is full.
So stay the fuck out of my head.

It could have gone a different way.
But you made your fucking bed.
Now I'm standing here full of rage.
And you don't care how much I've bled.

Coming undone so quietly
Nobody even knows.
They don't want to hear anyway
That's just the way it goes.

Same old story
Different day.
I need these demons
To go away.

There's nothing to be done
Nowhere to go.

Most of the time I don't
Even want anyone to know.

- *the contradiction of depression*

All the promise that I used to have
It's all gone and I can't get it back.
Dark and grey is the sky overhead
I've always known I'd be better off dead.

Childhood. Innocence. So far away.
Replaced by only shades of grey.

Barely a rhyme left in my head,
I've always known I was better off dead.

- *Where did I go?*

Games

Blinding hatred,
All consuming.
I barely know
What I'm doing.

The sight of the blood,
The sting of the blade,
Erases the memories
Of the games that we played.

I don't remember.
I'll never know.
Not sure if that's good,
None of it shows.

Told me not to
I went right ahead.
But sometimes I wondered
If I'd end up dead.
Buried underground
While you got off scot free.

> *Sometimes these thoughts*
> *Still catch hold of me.*

Told me what to do
I said no fucking way.
I wasn't ever sure I'd live
To see another day.
Stabbed in the back
While you're off living your life.

> *Sometimes I still see images*
> *Of you with a knife.*

Already Gone

Am I a dead heart walking
Or the walking undead.
All these people around me talking,
Nothing but numb in my head.

If I'm already gone
Does it even matter?
Can't see anything around me,
And I can't hear the chatter.

The world is irrelevant
And I'm already half gone.
I probably won't even
Finish this song…

Stuck

It's clear to me now,
Nothing's ever going to change.
Forever stuck in that room,
With nothing but rage.
One orange wall,
With a bright yellow cat,
I'm sixteen forever,
But I still can't go back.

Living in the past,
Fairytale world.
Nothing ever lasts,
Always that little girl.

- *Trapped in bubbles of time #2*

Not A Home

A house is not a home
If it tears you into pieces.
Rips flesh from the bone,
The pain only increases.

A house is not a home
If you're walking over landmines.
Already too far gone,
No stable ground to find.

A house is not a home
If it rips away your soul.
Tears apart your bones
And prevents you from being whole.

I would collect the dead bodies of rodents
and keep them delicately in plastic containers,
As if trying to grow life back into them,
Like I was the sun and they were the flower.

I would steal birds from their mothers
and think I was saving them,
Not understanding that some things
Need to *stay* with their parents
To *survive*.

- *liberation or subjugation?*

Rain

They don't see,
I never learn.
Too many choices,
Too many missed turns.

History only repeats and repeats
Until I can't stand the strain.
So I block it out with the musical beats,
While I stand in the rain.

She **slashed** her wrists
And *b l e d o u t* in the bath.
The pretty *d e a d* girl
Had the last **laugh**.

- *never letting this one go, <u>asshole</u>*

Living in the past.
Fairytale world.

Nothing ever lasts.
Always that little girl.

                                                      Tired of the lie
                                            Why can't I just die?

                                            Done with the pain
                                              I'm going insane.

Over and Over

Over and over again,
Same old stupid day.

Repeating history,
Put me out of my misery.

All the things they said,
Still stuck inside my head.

What's the point in trying
When I still only feel like dying?

Over and over again,
Same old stupid week.

Repeating history,
It's such a fucking mystery.

Why do all the things they said,
Still run rampant in my head?

I think people think I'm lying
When I tell them I am trying.

Over and over again,
I just do my best.

Over and over again,
Life puts me to the test.

Psycho girl.
Can't cope with the world.

Scars on her arms.
Keeps doing more harm.

Only one way out of this hell,
If only I could be someone else.

Feel seventeen again.
Can never share that pain.

- *Trapped in bubbles of time #3*

Fuck tryna make **amends**

I'd rather just have **revenge**

K

They might not see,
But I sure do.
The fucking demon
That resides in you.

                        Thought it would kill me
                              But I got out.
                          Not without wounds
                      And a whole lot of doubt.

                                        Don't know how I survived you,
                                              Though I'll never be whole.
                                           You fucked me up in the head
                                   And wounded me deep in my soul.

I hope you die,
And I'm not sorry for that.
Go to fucking hell,
And never come back.

Moments in time
Take over my mind.
No way to move on,
Never feel strong.

Over and over,
The things in my head.
Make me feel seventeen
Wishing I was dead.

More fresh cuts,
Still stuck in this rut.
Can never escape far away,
Still running forever and a day.

- *Trapped in bubbles of time #4*

Way of the World

They build us up
Just to knock us back down.
Stars in our eyes fading
As we fall to the ground.

Children so happy and bright
Falling fast as they grow bigger
And then out goes their light.

Spend the time wanting to be older
But no one ever warns you
That when you do, the world only gets colder.
Then you waste time wishing you could go back
And you're stuck in a moment
Thinking of all the things that you lack.

They tell you you'll have stars in your eyes,
But they tie you down
So you can never reach the sky.

No Forgiveness

Their faces still haunt me,
As I struggle through the days.
I've never been free,
Still stuck in this maze.

They all moved on,
And left me behind.
Never took me along,
Still so unkind.

Forgetting,
Their final unkindness.
Forgotten,
And I offer no forgiveness.

Whiskey Crying

All that whiskey crying
Didn't do you any good.

Stopped you from treating us all
The way that you should.

All your whiskey crying
Pushed me to my knees.

I felt like I was dying.
Stop this, stop this, please.

Overdramatic

I'm not trying to be overdramatic
But it's nearly 5 am,
And I'm lying here hating you
For making me love you again.

Why do I always want what I can't have?
Why do you have what you don't want?
Who are you to stay in my head,
Like it's one of your frequent haunts?

I may be a little overdramatic
But I'm sleep deprived as hell.
And I'm wandering through life
Trying to find my wishing well.

I say I want what I can't have,
But do I really want it?
I think it's just a smokescreen
To fence in all the things that haunt me.

I have always been too tightly wound,
I have never been a part of the crowd.
Nobody ever told me they were proud,
I have always felt more lost than found.

Ocean's Daughter

I sat and I stared out across the water
When I was sixteen I wanted to be the ocean's daughter.
I wanted to swim away from this horrible place
Put distance between myself and the pain.
All I could feel was the neverending space
Between me and the rest of the world.
Nowhere to run to and nowhere to go
All that I needed was somewhere that felt like home.

Under the sea,
Sounds good to me.
Let me go.
Sink beneath the foam.

I sit and I stare out over the water,
The little girl I used to be is now the ocean's daughter.
She swam away from that horrible place,
She no longer feels all that crippling pain.
All she feels now is the neverending peace,
All she feels now is that sweet release.
I'm still stuck here on land but she's under the water.
That little girl is finally the ocean's daughter.

Broke

You're sitting in the hallway of your grandparents house,
Everybody else is in the living room laughing and it feels so far away.
You're sad and you don't know why but no one notices.
If they do, they don't let on, and you're left sitting there alone.

You're lying in your old bedroom in your grandparents house
Footsteps on the stairs, your grandfather thinks you're on drugs.
If you weren't so disconnected you might have given him a hug.
But your eyes are dead, the way that you feel deep inside
Your whole life has been spent looking for yet another place to hide.

You're hiding in your wardrobe, fetal position,
Praying you don't hear those footsteps on the stairs.
Nowhere to really run, nowhere you can hide.
Nobody you can talk to because you don't think that they care.

Wondering where you went wrong.
What broke?
What broke it?
What broke **you?**

WHO *broke* <u>you?</u>

Teeth

Thoughts of death crowd your mind
from the time you're only eight years old,
Deep inside of you there are secrets
that don't ever want to be told.
Dark truths that the people who surround you
would never believe.
Except for the ones who did it to you,
who wear their teeth on their sleeve.

The Devil

The devil is real, I've seen him in his eyes
The devil is real, you shouldn't be surprised.

The devil is real, he's at the bottom of the bottle
The devil is real, the terrain he's in is hostile.

The devil is real, I see him in the mirror
The devil is real, he'll drown you in the river.

The devil is real, he's in the mind of a father
The devil is real, he's in the eyes of a daughter
The devil is real, he leads the lambs to slaughter.

The devil is real.
How does that feel?

Change

I used to sit and stare out at the rain.
                Waxing poetic in the moonlight.

Life drove me absolutely insane
                And I lost all of the will to fight.

I used to sit alone on a swing
                Staring up at those stars.

I never understood this thing,
                Happiness just felt too far.

Now I sit and stare up at the moon,
                Thinking about things so strange.

Things feel still, then gone so soon.
                One moment to the next, things change.

Bully

He pushed her down into the dirt
And raised his fist to make it hurt.
I stood in shock, he turned away,
We lived to fight another day.

We were never anything more
Than a little laughter
In an almost empty bar.
A scene set to disaster
As we scratched out all the stars.
Now it's kind of poetic
And I have locked that door.
And I don't find it so pathetic,
That you and I are nothing more.

- *Oh, Danny Boy*

Your Turn To Die

Making everyone believe your lies,
      The time has come for you to die.
No more tears left for me to cry,
      Time is up - now say goodbye.

Everybody believed your lies
      I'm so glad we said goodbye.
I have no more tears to cry,
      Careful, it's your turn to die.

I never believed your lies,
      I'm telling you for the last time.
Now it's your turn to die,
      I'm walking away with no goodbye.

Secrets

I kept the secret locked up tight
Like I've done my whole damn life.

All my secrets locked up tight
Where they've been my whole damn life.

I keep the secrets hidden away,
They're still there every single day.

I kept the secret hidden away,
I'll never tell, you'll never say.

How did you think I would react?
Did you really think I wouldn't fight back?
Day after day after fucking day,
You made me feel like I couldn't stay.

I can only hope that now you've grown
But even back then, you should have known.
I didn't deserve any of that shit
And I shouldn't have to shoulder all of it.

The words sometimes cut through like knives
And I sit on my own, wondering why.
Maybe there really isn't a reason,
Maybe you had nothing to believe in.

But I will try to be strong,
And I'll just keep moving on.
While your memory fades,
Though you may never fully go away.

- *untitled*

You look at pictures of yourself from the past. You're skinny. Beautiful. You didn't realise it at the time and you're angry at yourself because now you're sitting here, older, uglier, fatter. You let yourself go to waste.

<u>Look again</u>

Those pictures of yourself from the past? You were anorexic. Bulimic. Depressed. Suicidal. Anxious. Self harming. Psychotic.

All is not as it seems. Maybe not even as you remember it now.

- *Rose coloured glasses.*

We Mourn

We mourn the girls we could have been,
Those girls who were so unseen.
We mourn the things that we could have done,
Think back on the times we didn't have fun.
Mourn all the lives that went unknown,
All the places you just couldn't call home.

We mourn the world we could have lived in,
The different routes our life could have taken.
We mourn for the little girls we used to be,
The children who used to be so happy.

We mourn the kids who grew up too soon,
All the times we tried to reach for the moon.
We mourn the things we never got to do.
We mourn those girls - but they're still in you.

She was staring down at the blood on her hands. The light in the room felt harsh and she was squinting down at the floor, gaze stuck on her muddy shoes.

It wasn't supposed to go down like this. It was supposed to end in flames, not knives.

The events leading up to this. To being in this bright, white room, cuffs rubbing wrists raw. These events were put into place twenty-four years ago. When the devil started his game.

"What's the first thing you remember?"

"Fire."

The cigarette between his dirty fingers made her feel sick as she pushed open the door and crept into the house, swaying drunkenly as she tiptoed past his sleeping form for the stairs. Clinging to the banister, her gaze went back to the lit cigarette, taking in the ash, the nearly finished glass of whiskey, the wet snores coming from his mouth. She dragged herself up the stairs, hoping that cigarette fell and lit the couch he was sleeping on, on fire. She hoped it engulfed the whole house in flames so she could finally be free.

The fireplace in the living room. The flames licking the logs that came from the woods up the top of the back garden.

Bonfire night in her old hometown. Black sky, big gloves and hats, large flames and fireworks.

The Bunsen burners in chemistry class in high school. Staring at the flame while the class chatters and whispers and gossips around her. Wondering if it would hurt to put your hand in. One day doing it, very quickly, and feeling nothing.

The lighter that she used to light her own cigarettes, as she walked the cold streets in a big coat. Feeling hopeless and puffing away just to rebel. Wondering if she should put the flame against the delicate skin of her thin wrists. Saving that for the razor blade but still always wondering about the fire.

The candles she would light in her room that would drive her mother crazy. The flame flickering upwards and burning the top of the bookcase she set them on.

"What's the last thing you remember?"

"Fire."

Flames beginning to eat up the couch. Chewing at the jeans on his leg, searing into flesh. The screaming. The swearing. The punch.

"What happened next?"

"I don't remember."

She woke up covered in blood. His body was in a heap by the fireplace.

Six word story: **Blood and handcuffs. I am safe.**

Danielle

Too late now
You're just another star.
Keep trying to reach out
But it's just too far.

I'm sorry for the road you took,
I should have taken a second look.

So much left to live for
So much left to do.
Now we're all meeting up again
To say goodbye to you.

What if I'd reached out,
What if I'd come through.
Could have found a way
To reach out and save you.

You've gone away,
The pain's been transferred.
I just keep wondering,
What were your last words?

Witch

Could have burned at the stake,
Could have drowned in the river.
Dreamed of burning you alive
And cutting out your liver.

Never burned at the stake,
Never drowned in the river.
Always thought I was a mistake,
Now that little girl, I forgive her.

Colours

When I was young I wore colours on colours,
When I grew up I wore black.
Sometimes I wished that I'd been born another
And sometimes I wish I could go back.
Now I am older I wear colours on colours,
Somehow I think that is progress.
Still sometimes I wish I had been born another,
But day by day I am conquering my distress.

If I could show you one little thing,
I would show you that you did not win.
Tied me to the stake
But I did not burn.
Pushed me in the lake
But I did not drown.
I cast my spell and rose up from the ashes,
Now you better run,
Because I'm out for blood.
Go, go, fast as you can
Or you'll end up under the mud.

- *I could bury you*

Growing Up

Growing up in a house full of laughter,
You feel like you can't say a thing.
Growing up around all this disaster
Can't breathe when they walk in the room.
Led down the hill like a lamb to the slaughter,
He's got you by the throat.
Day after day, trying to tread water,
All that he does then is gloat.

Watches you drown,
Pushes you down.
Kills you without a frown.

Growing up with people all around you
But nobody with whom you can talk.
Growing up with seams that are coming unglued,
Can't find a stable bridge to walk.
Eyes on you when you walk in the room,
You want them to all go away.
Unhappy girl who will be gone so soon,
Too hurt to want to stay.

Watches you burn,
Smashes your urn,
Refuses to give you a turn.

Multicoloured child,
Where did you go?
Who drove you away,
Little rainbow girl?

Corrie

Never called you back,
And I regret that.
Misunderstandings ruin everything.
Now I won't ever see you again.

The stars were shining overhead
I don't remember everything you said,
But I remember it was something else.
We shone like those stars above.
And just for that one night
We were in love.

You were nothing but a stranger
Only spent one night together,
Who knew I'd still be here thinking of,
The way that it was.

Now you're an angel up above
But for the rest of my life,
I'll be in love.
With our one night.

Time

The years pass you by,
All you do is cry,
And you take it all out on yourself.
Time passes on,
You cry another song,
And you box it all up on the shelf.

The months pass you by,
You just want to fly,
And get away, find somewhere else.
Time passes on,
On silver wings I have flown,
'Cause I had to look after myself.

The days pass you by,
All I did today was cry,
And I took it all out on myself.
Time passes on,
I cried yet another song,
Tore apart all the books on my shelf.

The years passed by
I learned not to cry,
And I lost many parts of myself.
Time passed on,
I stopped writing songs,
And ignored all the books on the shelf.

Dead

I wished he was dead,
I wished I'd never bled,
I tore apart pieces of me.

I wanted him dead,
Off with his head,
Throw his body into the sea.

He didn't die,
I didn't cry.
Whatever,
Big fucking deal.
I didn't die,
He didn't cry.
Whatever,
Now let me heal.

My Body

I turn my head away
So they won't see,
All the little things
That I hate about me.

My body has changed
Over the years.
Happens when we've aged.
And I've cried too many tears.

Starved and binged,
Screamed and sinned.
Clawed my whole body away.

Then I brought it back,
But it felt like too much,
With my body, I've always felt out of touch.

Leave it alone,
Let the wind blow.
Who the hell cares what it looks like?
Let it grow,
Let it go,
Stop trying to put up a fight.

Perfection isn't your bones,
Perfection cannot be owned.
It's an illusion, it isn't real.
It's not something you can steal.

My body has carried me through war zones.
My body is my strongest home.

Picnic Bench

Sitting at a picnic bench
Crying my eyes out.
That poor, silly little girl,
All she ever did was shout.
But no one ever heard a thing,
Her mouth had been zipped shut.
She scribbled words on paper
To try and heal her bloody guts.

That House

Said "I'm not going back to that house"
But nobody heard a word.
Sent me back to my own private hell
With no care of how it would hurt.

Standing on the street that night,
Terrified and cold.
Better than going back to that house,
Where my secrets lay untold.

Still, I went back to that house,
Had nowhere else to go.
No one but me to save me;
That house is not a home.

Walking through the street that night,
You pushed, I pulled, we got in a fight.

I laughed, you joked, we sat on the ground,
It felt like something special had been found.

He thought we'd known each other forever,
This is the end of our endeavour--

But **how**, when it was just the beginning….

- cruel world

In My Head

Hiding in my cupboard,
Hiding under my bed.
Wishing I could be louder
Than the monsters in my head.

No one else can hear them,
Only I know they're there.
Though if I were to tell anyone
Would they even care?

Hiding in the cupboard,
HIding under the bed,
Will I ever be stronger
Than the demons in my head?

They called you a witch
So you called them a bitch
And wanted to tear their heart out.
Punch them in the gut
While you scream and you shout.
Stomp them into the ground
Leave them there,
Crying without a sound.

                         - *witches and bitches*

Day After Day

Walking for miles,
Tiring myself out.
Wondering what the hell,
This life is all about.

Sitting in my room,
Hiding myself away.
Colours all around me
But in my head, only grey.

Day after day,
Each one the same.
Day after day,
Nothing seemed to change.

None of you asked
Why I was crying.
None of you cared
That inside I was dying.

                     - *curled up in a sleeping bag*

The Forest

There's nothing to fear in the forest,
That's what they want you to think.
Take a deep breath, take a big step,
You're gone before you can even blink.

Danielle's Dead.

The news hit us like a freight train. Spreading through social media like an infectious disease. *Dead*. Danielle was dead.

When someone dies, it's kind of funny how many people come out of the woodwork. There were posts for miles and miles talking about how beautiful and amazing she was. Which was true. But Danielle could also be frustrating and exhausting, just like the rest of us. She was *human*. She was *depressed.* That's why she did it, you see. Danielle killed herself last night and nobody could be bothered to reach out far enough before it came to that point.

Or maybe that's not fair. Maybe people reached out as far as they could. Everyone has a different reach. One day you could be capable of less than you would be the next day. Less sympathy. Less empathy. *Less.*

Danielle needed *more.* People told her she was beautiful all over social media. They told her she wasn't fat, They made it known she could talk to them. Sometimes that stuff just isn't enough. Sometimes nothing can change what's inside.

Hours previously, Danielle had been laughing. That didn't mean a thing. Laughing didn't solve her problems or make them go away. She died anyway.

When I saw the news that morning, I felt drunk. I don't think I believed it. It felt wholly and utterly surreal. Once again it was brought home just how easy it was for someone to be here one minute and then gone the next.

I remember staring up at my bedroom ceiling for a few moments, all bleary-eyed and miserable. Waking up was always the worst part of the day. Coming back to consciousness, you were ripped from the escape of dreams (providing you hadn't had nightmares of course). Back to reality. And reality wasn't something I often wanted to come back to. A little like Danielle, I suppose.

It took a while to force myself upright. I would have muttered to myself as my dog came running up to greet me, to tell me to get the fuck up and walk him. I kept checking my phone. It had completely blown up, worming its way through everybody's socials. Snaking its ugliness into our lives.

I felt lifeless. I felt numb. I got up, I got dressed, I walked the damn dog. Music turned up, blocking out the world the way I had done since I was fifteen. At twenty six, it would have been a good idea to try and find some new coping mechanisms but I've really never been good at that. Which would prove itself again as one of my coping mechanisms of Danielle's suicide was to stop taking my antipsychotics cold turkey.

(Word of warning - not a good idea. Do not do this.)

I was completely struck by how life…. went on. Someone stopped moving, stopped laughing, stopped talking, stopped breathing… and everything and everyone that had been a staple in their life… didn't.

The world kept turning.

Danielle's dead. Danielle's dead.

The words kept going round and round in my head but I couldn't really seem to believe it. Sometimes I still can't. I *think* the words. Over and over and over again. They're there. They just don't always register properly. How can someone just not be there anymore?

Danielle was beautiful and funny. Alive and warm. She was so talented. She had moods like the rest of us but that didn't take away her light. That didn't make her any less important. She shone so brightly, I just wish she could have seen it for herself. I wish that I had done more to make her see it.

You can't change what's happened. You can't go back and start over. You can't tell someone they matter once they're gone. You just have to try and remember to do it while they're still here. But even when that doesn't work… you have to remember that it's not your fault.

You can't love someone back to life.

The Truth Will Set You Free

Said the truth will set you free,
I just rolled my eyes.
That stuff's really not for me
But now I realise:

No matter who said it,
The words ring true.
I regained my freedom
When I opened up to you.

The truth will set you free.
Never thought that was true for me.
It was a nice sentiment,
Wrapped up in a ribbon.
Presented to me like a gift.
I never imagined that I could shift
The heavy weights that held me down.
But now I look up at the sky
And part of me feels proud.

Said the truth will set you free,
I just rolled my eyes.
Now I'm finding my way back to me
And I think I realise.

Cigarette smoke and
the smell of whiskey
cling to me
just like the ghosts of
your claw-like fingers,
nails still
scratch, scratch, scratch-ing
away the parts
of me that survived.

Night Terrors

The room stretched for miles,
And you lay there in terror.
Just a scared little child,
Unsure of the horror.

Ghosts danced around your bed,
Chanting words you don't remember.
Their faces trapped inside your head,
From January to December.

Some kind of Alice in Wonderland syndrome,
Any feelings of safety thrown out the window.

Night terrors.
Help, Alice!
The room stretching out,
The chanting all around.
Round and round
Dizzying heights.
Lost and found,
Blinded by the lights,
Falling without a sound.

Alice in Wonderland.
Give me your hand.
Everything's bigger
Then everything's smaller,
I can't reach the door
Then I'm ten feet taller.

Night terrors
Or ghosts?
Which one
Would be better?
Am I dreaming
Or just haunted?
Maybe they're the same thing.

I searched for you
Before I knew,
Just where your loyalty lies.
Can't say I was surprised,
You just ruined my perfect fairytale.
Hammered in another rusty nail.

I looked for you
Before I knew,
I didn't need someone to rescue me.
Don't care if I never see
Your face for the rest of my life,
I rescued myself, pulled me back from those heights.

- *I don't want to know you*

Dani

Your laugh was the loudest I'd ever heard,

      I wish you didn't feel unloved in this world.

So many people cared about you,

      More than you probably ever knew.

Five Years (Plus Fourteen)

I remember thinking five years
Was a massive hill to climb.
I remember all the tears
That I had to cry.

Now it's been nineteen years.
What the fuck?
Don't know how I ended up here.
Strength or luck?

Still can't let the images go,
But they're more faded
Than they were before.
And I'm not quite as jaded
As I was.

Five years, plus fourteen,
I've come through the other end.
Not sure what that means,
But I think I'm on the mend.

I remember laughter and jokes.
I remember sometimes feeling outside of it.
I remember grown ups and alcohol and cigarette smoke..

I remember Christmas and Boxing Day.
I remember sometimes not feeling part of it.
Like an outsider.

I remember wishing it was over.

Then I remember missing it when it was gone.

Stormy Weather

Is it a weakness

If I can't slit my wrists?

Am I getting better,

Or just delaying stormy weather?

Princess

Once, there was a princess
locked away in her tower.
Held captive by a wicked king
alone without any power.

Once, there was a princess
who lost her precious prince.
The wicked witch took him away,
and she hasn't seen him since.

Once, there was a princess
who hid herself away.
Locked herself up in a brand new tower,
didn't want to face another day.

Once, there was a princess
who bravely took a step.
Walked right through a deadly fire,
to face what she had left.

I sit and I stare,

Every day, at the screen.

It builds up inside me,

A long, howling scream.

- *was I the wolf all along?*

Strong

Time and time and time again,
I lose my hope and all my friends.

Keep getting up, keep going on,
I think that's all you need to be strong.

No matter how many times you fall,
Just keep going through it all.

You've Got To Love You

To go around hating what you are,
This isn't good, you've come so far.
So why are you still walking around,
With your head up in those darkened clouds?

Don't cry your heart out,
Don't close your eyes now.
Raise your eyes from the ground
Stand up, take a good look around,
You're everything special, and everything real
I don't understand why you said what you said
I don't understand why that goes round in your head.

I know the truth,
You've got to love you.

Fly Away

Feels much worse than it really is
The pain you caused, never felt nothing like this.
Lies flying back and forth, can't even think
No other choice but to let myself sink.

And you don't know anything.
And I don't want you to anyway.

Gonna fly away, get away, leave tonight,
Do a runaway, catch a train, out of sight.
Don't bother following, I don't wanna see your face
Just let me fly away.

The sun was shining on the grass
And I ignored your evil eyes.

The ferocity of my aggression
Took everybody by surprise.

I couldn't take the darkness
that you brought into my life.

I'd had enough with all the torture
so I put you aside.

- *goodbye*

Once upon a time, there was a girl. Isn't there always a girl? She lived in a little town where nothing interesting ever happened and no one of interest ever came to. She was ruled over with an iron fist by her evil stepfather. The girl longed to escape the town, her stepfather, her life. You and I both know, however, that it is never as easy as longing for something. A longing is never enough to change a life. To make it better. There are no Gods watching over us, listening to our cries for help, and if there are Gods... they do not act. They sit and listen to our pain and our cries, and they do nothing.

The little town where the girl lived was full of people who did not understand her. They would point and whisper and gossip. She was different, you see. She didn't know *how* she was different but she knew that she *was*. Why else would she be treated so poorly? Why would she be ostracised? Why would she feel so alone?

Then, one day, the girl found a book. A magic book. A book full of wonder and hope and a whole new life just waiting for her. Calling to her. The girl loved books and she loved to read, it was an escape. Maybe this was another reason why the people of the town whispered so much about her. They weren't all as crazy about books as she was. Maybe they had nothing to escape, she thought, though this wasn't true. We all know that everybody has something they wish to escape. Something they're running away from.

The only way that she could escape from the clutches of her evil stepfather was to jump headfirst into the book. Run away into the pages. What was once a metaphorical occurrence turned into a literal experience. The girl was whooshed away, transported to a magical land. The realm of fairy tales. However, these are not the fairy tales of our world. These are the true stories, the ones that really happened. The lives of Cinderella and her Prince are a lot different than we've been led to believe, as the girl would soon find out.... *even fairy tales can't always be perfect.*

Fairy Tales. Instagram. Celebrity.
Perfection is an unattainable fantasy.

My **body** has *carried* me through **war zones**.

I **owe** a *lot* to it.

It doesn't **matter** what it *looks like*.

It is <u>**strong**</u>.

Scars

Please don't be alarmed,
By the scars on my arms.

They are the constellation I followed,
The visions and voices; they swallowed.

The stars that lit my way,
What helped me to stay.

Didn't feel like it at the time,
But it was necessary to survive.

These thin silvery lines
Taking me one day at a time

Food

Food is necessary for survival,
Don't live your life dead on arrival.
You don't need to see every bone,
Don't fall for what those pictures show.
Instagram isn't real, it's fake,
Never let it make you forsake
Your health.

Food is necessary for survival,
Don't force your body into deprival.
You don't need to see every bone,
Those voices are lying to you, you know.
Don't beat yourself up for every bite,
It really isn't important what you look like.

Look after your body and your mind,
Filter out all the voices, so unkind.
Food is needed to survive,
Not for looks, but to stay alive.
Block out all that perfection shit,
Food is not the enemy - please don't fight it.

*I'm
proud
I'm
still
here*

*you
should
be
too*

Good Old Days

Passing out on living room floors,
All of us wishing we could be much more.
Drunk and laughing, we were so young,
None of us knew what was to come.

I thought you'd all be with me forever,
I should have learned my lesson that friendships sever.
I loved you all then and I love you now,
Even though you're no longer around.
It's funny how time makes things fade away,
But I'll always fondly look back on our good old days.

Laughing in the streets 'till 3 am,
All of us, the best of friends.
Enemies and lovers, we were it all,
Writing our own story, never thought we'd fall.

I thought you'd all be with me forever,
You think by now I would've been more clever.
I loved you all then and I love you now,
Though sometimes I wish you were still around.
It's funny how time can make the memories fade,
Still, I'll always look back fondly on our good old days.

Best Friends

Me and Sarah
Were so young when we were together.
Little kids taking on the world.
Hiding under tables, laughing with each other.
Bridesmaids dresses; The Lion King; no insults hurled.
Never thought I would ever need another.

Me and Amy
Used to run around causing trouble,
In the village we used to live.
Her and me, in our own little bubble,
Gave her all I had to give.
Spending every day together,
Those were the best days of my life,
Thought that we would be best friends forever.

Me and Yasmin
Used to write our own little songs.
Still remember every word of that chorus.
With her, I felt like I could belong,
So much fun, just the two of us.
Drifted apart, I suppose,
But don't you know
That's just the way life goes.
"Wherever you go, whatever you do,
You know I will be standing
RIght beside you."

Me and Laura
We were pretty crazy kids,
The woods were somewhere
We would practically live.
Lord of the Rings was our happy place,
Almost every day with her
Was spent with a smile on my face.
Lost her at the end but she came back,
True friend in the end,
She has a courage that I lack.

Me and Kimberley
Were as close as you could be.
She was my angel,
She was like a sister to me.
Loved her then and I love her now,
Though it's been a while since I've seen her around.

Me and Paula
What the hell can I say?
She was the fucking coolest,
It was the two of us every day.
Skipping school and getting up to mischief.
She was so much braver than me.
She stole my sadness away like a thief.
Broke my heart when she did what she did.
Now I keep all that locked up tight,
Don't like to lift that lid.

Me and Adele
We would talk every single day,
She was my saviour
In so many different ways.
Don't think I was *her* best friend
But she sure was one of mine,
I really thought that it would never end
Somehow, without her, I went on fine.

Me and Lynne
Were the coolest duo ever.
Fox 'n' Finn,
We were going to be that way forever.
Reached for the stars
We had so many plans.
Our paths changed after we fell apart,
And I know the fault was mine.
She still has a piece of my heart
And I hope that she's doing fine.

Me and you,
You and me,
We grew up together.
Really thought that we would be best friends forever.

Insincere

Your insincere apologies,
They don't fool me.

You could have the whole world on your side,
And I still would not give up this fight.

This thing has gone too far now,
And I just don't see any way out.

I'm never going to give in
And you're never going to win.

This has gone on far too long,
I'm sick of writing these same old songs.

Your insincere apologies
Will never mean a thing to me.

Bedale

The water of the beck
Was travelling downstream.
The sun was shining in the sky,
Prettiest blue I'd ever seen.

The ducks were swimming,
And this was living.

Bonfire night out at the park,
Standing there in the cold and the dark,
Watching the pretty colours light up the sky,
Feeling so free it was almost like I could fly.

The sparklers were sparkling,
And this was the best thing.

Riding my bike all over town,
Pedaling without a care.
Sunshine, grey clouds,
Whatever weather, you'd find me there.

The pond at the primary school,
Looking for frogspawn like it was jewels.

Little places I used to go,
I remember it all so clearly.
Might never walk any of those streets again,
But I'll always love that little town dearly.

An envelope shaped necklace,
Never will I forget this.
.

From The Ground Up

Building myself
From the ground up.
Don't know how
I ended up so stuck.
But I'm clawing back
The pieces of myself,
That people tore away.

The parts of my being
That got lost along the way.
Wonder, if I had kept them,
Where I would be today.
That doesn't matter,
No use in dwelling
On the secrets in me
That I'm still not telling.

Despite all of this,
I'm figuring out.
Just what the hell
This whole thing is about.
Can live with what's inside,
Just have to accept.
The evil inside me,
Has no power left.

Writing

I keep writing myself in circles,
Keep tying myself up.
Knots upon knots of words,
Songs I've never heard.

Am I writing to find myself?
Or am I writing to get it out?
Am I writing myself to pieces,
Screaming without a sound?

I keep writing myself in knots,
Etching words into my skin.
Spilling out all of my thoughts,
And all the things I hold within.

It's impossible,
Like moonbeams in the morning sun.

It's horrible,
Like angels turning into demons.

Harry

I don't know what you've been up to
During all these years that have passed.
But I still recall you fondly,
Trust me, your memory did last.

Well, I hope that you've been doing well
And I hope that you've been happy.
It's a shame I'll probably never get to tell
You how much you helped me.

You never had a bad word to say,
And could always put a smile
Upon my face each and every day.

I wonder if you ever spared a thought for me,
In all these years since I had to leave..
Did you keep that old job or did you pack it in?
I still have that note you wrote, I read it now and then.

And even when it was all gone,
All these memories still lived on,
You would not believe,
The impact that you had on me.

The words used to flow from me like raindrops from the sky,
Been dried up for years now, and frozen in time.

Pieces of myself fragmented and chipped away,
Was living on borrowed time every damn day.

Used to have a light, that would shine so bright,
But they ripped it away from me night after night.

Screaming so loud without even making a sound,
Lying on a trampoline in the dark, staring up at the clouds.

The stars shining a hundred light years away,
Wishing the sky would swallow me up and take me away.

Train's coming down the tracks and you don't even care,
Don't look right or left, it misses you by a hair.

                                  - *little fragments passing by*

Triumph

How quick a triumph turns into a tragedy.
How quickly we fall down for everyone to see.
How easily we bruise,
When we think we have nothing left to lose.

Look down, before you fall.
Look out, don't wanna lose it all.

Maze of Time

Sometimes I catch my mind wandering,
Heading back through the long maze of time.
I'll find myself in the spring of 2007,
Where I was feeling anything but fine.

There you are,
There you stand.
You're reaching out,
You take my hand.

You ask how I've been sleeping,
Wondering how I've been feeling.
"Not good, not great," is my reply.
It was all I could do not to cry.

Prayed for me,
But I couldn't see
Any way out,
I couldn't stop looking down.

Sometimes I catch my mind wandering,
Heading back through the long maze of time.
I'll find myself in many different places,
Not many of them I remember feeling fine.

Can I find my way out of this maze,
Or will I be stuck for the rest of my days?

Friend

Thought I couldn't breathe without you,
But I'm doing just fine.
Thought I couldn't live without you,
But it's better with you gone.

You never really were a friend,
Right up to the bitter end.
Never there when I needed you,
Though I always came running.

Pathetic little outbursts
Just to get your attention,
Well, whatever, I'm done with you
And all your fake affection.

Spreading my secrets all over town,
Pretending to be little miss innocent.
Well, honey, life without you here is just fine,
I should've done this years ago.

Eighteen years have come and gone,
Almost to the day.
I have sang song after song,
I have lived through all the rain.

22nd of October always stops me in my tracks.
Just for a moment as my mind travels back.

- *don't think your eyes will ever leave my head*

Still Working

I've been staying up 'till five am,
Losing myself in fear again.
Searching through old memories,
Trying to find the missing parts of me.

I lost pieces of me on the way,
Little things I wish had stayed.
The music and the words were all I had.
Over time, I felt it all fade to black.

Once a piece of gold,
Now a faded piece of brass.
Forever lost my shimmer,
Like a broken shard of glass.

It kind of seems like
I'll never really stop hurting.
Been bruised and broken,
But look - I'm still working.

Lying Here Tonight

Let the rain pour down on me.
When it's gone, I'll regain clarity.

I see grass growing greener on the other side
I can just reach out and touch it, lying here tonight.

Devastating emotional damage
Keeps hitting me deep inside.
Help me put an end to the carnage,
I no longer want to hide.

I hope you sat there disappointed,
Bet you stared at your phone, thoughts disjointed.
Grab another drink, tonight's on me.
I'm done playing this game, you see.

It was raining boy,
It was pouring down.
Then just yesterday your sarcastic smile
Helped me turn it back around.

The grass is still growing greener on the other side,
But the sky is so much clearer where I'm lying here tonight.

Too Late Now

Sunshine memories.
Another cold February.
You and me together,
Think it could have been forever.

I kept on pushing you away,
You never backed up.
Never really gave you a reason to stay.
Never gave you enough.

Walking through the bus station hand in hand.
You and I in a drunken wonderland.

Sitting down by the water.
An aquarium visit.
You loved an unknown man's unknown daughter.
But it's too late now. Isn't it?

Mistakes

Every one of us has made mistakes,

But how much of this can one person take?

You try and you try but nothing ever works,

I cry and I cry but I can't get out of the dirt.

Haunt You

What they tell me, I just can't see,
Hate everything to do with me.
Weakly, pathetically losing my mind,
Searching for something that I can't find.

Everything hurts now, I can't even breathe.
Would you spare a thought for me if I should leave?

What if I died young,
Would the thought stay with you?
Would you start listening then?
What would you do?
All the warning signs
That you never paid heed to.
On a cold December night,
They'll probably haunt you..

Undone

I think I'm starting to lose my mind,
I'd listen to you but your words are unkind.
Open your eyes but keep your mouth closed,
Don't pretend to understand when you don't know.

I'm gonna run a line across a railway track,
Race across that bridge and never look back.

Look what you've done, look what you've done.
Can't be undone, can't be undone.

Run away. Get out of town.
Start again. Get rid of the frown.

All of the <u>chances</u>
That I ***didn't*** take.
The washed up *romances*,
And **cruel twists** of <u>fate</u>.

Rollercoaster Ride

I'm crying every single day,
Haven't smiled a real smile for ages.
I find myself staying up all night
Wishing that everything would be alright.

All I need is a hand to steady me when I fall,
What I need is somebody who won't judge me at all.
I can't feel anything, my head is so numb,
You can tell that I ain't gonna be too much fun.

Sorry for the rollercoaster ride,
Just promise you'll still be here when I open my eyes.

Agoraphobia

Outside makes my head spin,
Never feels like I can win.
Too much space all around me,
Tunnel vision, all I can see.

People everywhere I go,
Though none of them will ever know
Their very presence is unsafe,
Why can't I be more brave?

Best of Days

Green grass,
Sunshine rays.
Those really were
The best of days.

Frogspawn,
Ripped jeans.
Whitest clouds
I'd ever seen.

Running water,
Sleepovers.
Exploring fields.
Four leaf clovers.

Secret hideouts,
Barbie dolls.
Scuffed knees
And close calls.

Barbecues,
Midnight haze.
These really were
The best of days.

Water has always been my safe place.

The beck in Bedale where I would walk along and sit beside and even venture into. Dipping my feet into the running water. Crossing barefoot to the other side. Watching the ducks and their ducklings. Skipping school and skipping stones.

The ocean in Spain where I would walk alone with my music turned up loud. Dipping toes into the waves. Peaceful in the dark.

The river on the way home from school where we would stop and drink. The water cool and refreshing and the sound gentle.

My secret hideout. Rocks by the water, behind the train track. Hidden from view and all alone. Safe with the water lapping up against the shore around me.

The shower I hide in at the end of a long or difficult day. The water cascading over me and shielding me like an invisible protective barrier. Washing away the dirt and the stress.

Water has always been a safe space.

Crazy

Crazy walking girl,
That's what they called me.
As if using your legs
Was strange.

Crazy witch girl,
That's what they called me.
As if finding comfort in nature
Was wrong.

Crazy,
They called me.
Crazy,
They called me.

Crazier still
Was their definition of crazy.

Crazy no matter what you do,
So just do whatever you want to.

Crazy walking girl,
Walking for miles.
Lost in her own world,
Where was her smile?

Crazy witch girl,
Collecting her crystals.
Stuck in her own world,
Anything to stay blissful.

You focused on the wrong thing,
And she kept on slipping.
All along, you were the crazy ones.
The scales keep on tipping.

Change

Feels like it won't ever change,
Destined to always be this strange.

Don't want to be the warning
That others must follow.
Just another cautionary tale,
While inside me is just hollow.

I've been in this place before,
Thinking I'd opened a better door.
Then I fell right back.
Will this be like that?

Help,
I'm screaming inside.
Help,
Please open your eyes.

Nothing's ever going to change,
Got to sleep in this bed I've made.

I used to be terrified
of horror movies
until I realised
I was in one
of my own.

- *I am the final girl*

Memory Lane

I'm looking at the pictures,
Taking it all in.
Big Me and Little Me walking down memory lane.

I watch my past through rose tinted glasses.
Romanticising the pain,
As I walk down memory lane.

Smile and laugh with tears in my eyes.
Flipping through each page.
Walking hand in hand with me down memory lane.

Boy & Girl

The one who was always there,
The one who always cared.

The bright, colourful boy
And the dull, scarred girl.
I never let you get close
To being in my world.

The one who always understood,
The one who always saw the good.

The bright, beautiful boy
And the sad, lonely girl.
I let you slip right through my fingers,
Because of all the ghosts that lingered.

The one who stayed through it all,
No matter how many times I'd fall.

Within

I feel like everyone can see it all over me.
I can feel it underneath my skin.
Clawing, scratching to get out,
Can feel it lurking there within.

They can see it all over my face,
All over my body, all over my soul.
I carry it with me from place to place,
It prevents me from ever being whole.

They can all read it in my thoughts,
It's written in the air around me.
I feel like I am caught,
Close my eyes, it's all I can see.

Can everyone see it all over me?
Can they see it clawing at my skin?
Scratching, biting, ripping, slashing.
Can everybody see it there within?

Somebody violates you
        and it writes itself into your soul.

The act sits upon your skin
        and burrows into your flesh.

Gnawing away pieces of you
        and turning you into something unrecognisable.

You look at your face in the mirror and
        it doesn't even look like you looking back.

You look up at the sky and the sun is shining
        but you can't even feel it.

It's like you're not even here.

You're not on this planet anymore.

You're not the same person anymore.

The pieces of you have been eaten away
        and shot up into the air.

Floating around you but not connecting
back with the broken parts and so
you feel like every time somebody looks at you
they are seeing all of those fragments.

You feel like it's written all around you
        in massive capital letters,
              easily readable by every single person you pass by.

Somebody violates you
        and it stitches itself into your flesh.

You are bloody gaping wounds
        and weeping pus.

But you are still here.
And you can rebuild.

Life

Friends come,
And friends go.
Seasons change,
In comes the cold.

Time moves,
Life changes.
Things improve,
Then it rages.

Grief and tears,
Laughter and smiles.
So many years.
So many miles.

People go,
And people come.
Seasons change,
Out comes the sun.

It was you and me
Against the world.
The two of us,
Careless girls.

It was me and you
Through the years.
Sleeping over
And sharing tears.

Bus rides and skipping school.
Studying on your living room floor.
Being your friend was so fucking cool,
Laughing and running out the door.

Through the trees,
You and me.
By the water,
Nothing but laughter.

Did what you did
And ruined it all.
Guess you had your own problems
But it was me you let fall.

You ruined it all,
Why'd you have to do that?
People aren't dolls.
And now we can never go back.

- *another one for you, paula*

With grace, beauty and poise,
She walked fearlessly through life.
Talented beyond measure,
A devoted mother and wife.

Never had the chance to meet,
But still we somehow grieve.
The ending's always bittersweet,
But people have to leave.

Lucky to have even just a minute,
And I know they'll make her proud.
Life may be hard without her in it
It's always tough when someone's not around.

She will never be gone.
Her memory won't fade
And her spirit will live on.
Be proud of the life she has made.

We get by.
And please remember,
It's okay to cry.
Her strength lives on
In all of you.
Put one foot in front of the other
Especially on the days you feel blue.

- *rip*

Today is a writing day so up goes the hair.
Kind of feel like Violet Baudelaire.

Under My Skin

I remember sitting in the back seat,
Music blasting in my ears.
Your eyes in the mirror staring back at me,
Another one of my biggest fears.

I remember we had seen a movie
About a truly evil man,
Who wanted to kill these children.
I really related you to that.

Now every time I play that album,
The one I had on in that car.
It transports me back to that moment
Though the years have brought me so far.

The memories come flooding back,
And that dark foreboding feeling.
Threatens to pull me right back in
But it's too late 'cause now I'm healing.

Still, the songs from Under My Skin,
Will hold those memories within.

Final Girl

Running through the trees,
Blood gushing from my skinned up knees.
Branches catching in my hair,
I look back; I know they're there.

There's nowhere else to go,
I'm holding my breath.
The blood continues to flow
As I think I'm close to death.

Then suddenly they're gone,
The world around goes silent.
I'm able to get up and move on,
Though I'll be haunted by the violence.

The final girl survives,
She always makes it out alive.
But it always comes with a cost,
Forever haunted by what she's lost.

I'm the final girl.
The last girl standing.

Going Strong

Sometimes it just hits you,
The years have flashed right by.
Suddenly you're ten years older
Looking up at the same sky.

The one you gazed towards
When you were just a child.
The years have stripped away
Everything innocent and wild.

But you are still here
And you're moving on.
Despite all of your fears,
You're still going strong.

When I was about eight years old
I took a pair of safety scissors to my hair
in the middle of the day at the back of class.

I threw it in the bin and hoped nobody would notice
but I still remember my teacher finding it
and holding it up to the hair of my redhead best friend,
trying to see who the colour matched.

I had dark brown hair.

It was slightly amusing that she would even try
to match it to the other girl,
whose hair was the fairest orange-gold.

I remember her figuring out it was me
and I remember crying.

For years afterwards
the children would whisper about it.

I remember hearing it
as I walked past to the bin to sharpen my pencil.

I remember shooting them a glare.

I remember wanting to cry
because nobody understood.

This was the start of me believing I was *crazy*.

Why did I do it?

Why did I take scissors
to my beautiful hair
in a classroom?

maybe because it had been tainted

diary entry - October 31st, 2010.

"Was going to wear a skirt today. Looked ridiculous. Back in jeans. Still look ridiculous."

diary entry - April 18th, 2021.

If I could go back I would tell her to wear the skirt. Life is too short and she looks amazing.

So wear the skirt. You look amazing.

Years have gone
More shall pass.
These tragic days
Won't be our last

Whiskey Bottle

The whiskey tasted sweet to him,

But bitter to everyone else.

He turned to the bottle every time

To tell it how he felt.

Only Friends When We're Drinking

When I see you now, I'm not filled with doubt
It feels like the two of us don't remember how to hang out.

We're only friends when we're drinking
So don't act like you didn't notice our ship was sinking.

We're only friends when it suits you
Only friends when it suits me too.

So let's not get swept away with the shame
Of all these broken memories we share.

I'd rather you didn't act like you know what I'm thinking
'Cause we're only friends when we're drinking.

Can't Stay

Going back to the city that I thought I knew,
Didn't think I'd make it, came out black and blue.
Happy Ever After might not be so far away,
Used to think I'd hate to go, now I know I can't stay.

                Don't pretend you're sad about it
                    We both know you're not.
                Don't pretend to be my friend now
                      Don't think I forgot.

I'll soon be free of this, of you, of everything,
You have no idea how much that makes me want to sing.
Never tell me what to do, I'll go the opposite way,
Don't think I care anymore, I know I can't stay.

*You find yourself
livin' for grey skies
starry nights
and elaborate lies.*

Ink

The ink that I've spilled over the years
Still ain't got a damn thing on my tears.
You can change the setting but the rest won't disappear,
I'll admit I'm not quite sure how I've lasted all these years.

The ink that I've spilled over the years
Stitches together every one of my fears.
You can move away but it doesn't disappear,
It follows you down every road for the rest of your years.

Friends

Friends aren't supposed to treat friends that way,
Do you really have nothing else to say?
I always knew you were no good,
Didn't think you'd tell me to my face.

And it was a shame that it ended
But I'm not sad that you're gone.
You can pretend that you don't notice
And I can keep sitting here alone.
But you and I are over now,
I really should have known.

Friends aren't meant to spread your stuff all over town,
Aren't they supposed to help you up when you fall down?

Friends have never been my
Greatest strength.
I always seem to turn around
And find that they have left.

Private Hell

The world is losing colour
As the numbness settles in.

t's remarkable how many emotions
Have gone missing from within.

I'm sitting here in silence,
An empty little shell.

I'm sitting here burning alive
In my own private hell.

Once I got in this mood
I always found myself
eager to stay this way.
I spent so much time
walking around feeling empty
that it was almost as if
being angry validated
my existence
in some strange way.

Drunk Words

They say that drunk words are sober thoughts
but I don't believe that to be true.
Every time I have been drunk and
started breaking down over you,

It was always something else
tearing at my mind.
The scrambled vodka sadness,
that I hid my truth behind.

Alcohol tears, for me
were nothing but a smokescreen,
I had so much darkness
and hid it behind things I didn't mean.

If I'm being honest,
I very often find myself annoyed
because I told you <u>anything</u> at all.

That's what I'm angry at most -
I'm angry at **myself**
for telling you <u>personal</u> details about my life.

I wish I could claw
the words back
into my throat
and tuck them
all the way down
into my toes

I think we all do that though

We leave pieces of ourselves
with other people
as we travel through our lives.

Truthfully,
other people
are too
focused
on themselves
to be overly
concerned with
keeping your
intimate confessions
in the forefront
of their mind.

Alcohol

There's whiskey in the glass,
The smell is in the air.
I feel like I want to throw up
As I walk up the stairs.

There's beer in the bottle,
There's smoke in the air.
It's tearing me apart
So I'm hiding up the stairs.

There was cider in my glass,
Laughter in the air.
Don't remember a thing
Before I staggered down the stairs.

There was vodka in my bottle,
Smoke in the air.
I walked out of the club,
Tripping down the stairs.

when I was young
the kids on my block
told me there was a ghost cat
in the woods behind our houses.

I believed it
without question.

the rest of my life
that ghost cat
travelled around with me.
in my head.

I never forgot
and I never let go.

why is that?

Hidden Girl

Hiding under tables
on boxing day,
shying away from
the grown ups.
Unable to run away.

Tucking herself away
into the drawers
under the bed.
Lying in the dark
surrounded by soft toys.

Somehow feeling peace,
the voices in my head cease.

Dancing in
snow globes,
curled up
in her wardrobe.

Hiding in the card shelf
of her grandparents corner shop.
Wanting to stay there
until everyone else forgot.

Hiding away in the park
hoping nobody came by.
Hiding in the dark,
comforted by stars in the sky.

I Have

I have lived a thousand lives,
I have cried a thousand times.

I have been stuck in reverse,
I have felt like I'm a curse.

I have climbed up every hill,
I have sat there, calm and still.

I have been a thousand things,
I have flown on sparkling wings.

I have conquered all my pain,
I have and I will again.

How can you grieve
For someone you've never met?
Is there some kind of link,
Do we all connect?

Alive

Found you in the dark,
You were a light to guide the way.
I know I took it too far,
Should have told you that day.

I'm sorry for the ride,
It was a pretty crazy time.
But the fact I can't deny,
In a way, you kept me alive.

Stuck in Blue

Some mornings I wake up,
And realise I have dreamt of you again.
It's funny how after all this time,
Your memory can still stir that old pain.

Somehow you and I are still connected,
I wonder if that means anything.
In my mind your blue eyes are still reflected,
Have to admit, the image still stings.

Some afternoons I sit there,
And think back on the you I knew.
Funny how after all these years,
I can still get stuck in blue.

My first memory of being called *stupid*
was when I was ten years old
and my teacher spat it at me across the room.

My last memory of being called *stupid*
was from your dirty mouth
as you spat it at my back before you shoved the knife in.

The War Is Over

be kind to the little girl you used to be.
she did her very best
to survive.

wrap her up in warm blankets.
tell her the war is over
and she's alive.

Growing Flowers

Thought we were growing flowers together
But in reality it was just me growing them with my tears.
Dreamed it would be you and me forever
But I ended up alone in the dark with my fears.

Now I'm happy growing flowers alone
Though the reality can be a little bittersweet,
Now I'm dreaming about where me and myself can go
The past and the present finally meet.

the way
he looked at her
was enough
to make me think
that maybe love
wasn't a complete lie
after all

- *they have to be faking it, right?*

Soldier

One bad soldier
Created another.
Threw her to the wolves,
And devoured her mother.

One bad soldier
Created a carbon copy,
Left her in the trenches
No grave marked with a poppy.

Ariel

You took my words
You took my sanity.
You took my voice
You took all clarity.

Like Ariel
I lost my voice
That hurt the most,
It was never my choice.

I took back my words,
I took back my sanity.
I took back my voice
I took back my clarity.

Like Ariel
I found my voice.
Regained a piece back
And now I can rejoice.

Special

Are you hurting someone else
Or am I just special?
All those things that I felt
And you'd just tell me I was mental.

Are you beating someone else down
Or am I a special case?
Unfortunately I think I've memorised
Every look upon your face.

You told the class that you pick up snails
from the pavement and move them
out of harm's way.

Fifteen years later, I still do the
very same thing.

with snails,
with bees,
with worms.

This is the impact people have
on our worlds without them
even knowing it.

                                              - *philosophy*

I should have asked you questions,
I should have spent more time.
I never seem to think about
What is on the line.

                    You regret the things you miss
                      But you hide yourself away.
                    Too much energy to reminisce,
                        Overhead the sky is grey.

                                      People go too quickly,
                                      In and out of your life.
                                You have to try and remember
                                We really don't have much time.

Am I a horror trope?
Have I lost all hope?
How did I even cope?
Is there anywhere to go?

There's spiders in my throat,
I'm beginning to choke.
I'm in a sinking boat.
I'm a fucking horror trope.

- *but am I the villain or the final girl?*

Little Red

On the way to Grandma's house,
Shortcut through the woods.
Snarling from over my shoulder,
I quickly tug up my red hood.

The silence here is deafening,
Something's in the air.
I'm starting to get the feeling
That something is out there.

On the way to Grandma's house,
Before I can even react,
The wolf is suddenly upon me,
Its claws are in my back.

He got me by the throat,
And I think I'm about to be dead.
I'm starting to choke,
It's the end of Little Red,

I'm buried underground now,
When suddenly I open my eyes.
Now I'm Little Dead Rotting Hood,
What a big fucking surprise.

Face The Truth

There always comes a time
When you have to face the truth.
You cannot run forever,
You can't just start anew.

No matter where you go,
The tangled strings follow.

Turn to face the demons
Biting at your heels.
No point in outrunning it.
The devil's made his deal.

There always comes a time
When you have to face the truth.
Your mind knows when it's ready.
The power lies in you.

Once upon a time there was a wicked sea witch. She was driven away into the depths of the ocean, hiding out in her cave, surrounded by sharks and stingrays.

She sat in her cave all day, casting spells. Casting curses onto those who had driven her away. Voodoo and black magic.

They had it coming, after all. The sea witch never used to be so wicked. She used to be a normal mermaid, swimming the ocean, playing with the fish and making jewellery out of coral.

Then the other mermaids played a cruel game.
They turned on her.
Laughed, taunted, jeered.
Pulled her hair and broke all of her jewellery.
Stole her pearls and smashed her collection of sea glass.

So she fled. The little mermaid was driven away from the kingdom to her cave, and she became the wicked sea witch. She collected seaweed and she cursed and cursed about the mermaids who had turned her into this monster.

She became bitter and hid away from everyone and everything, relying on black magic to get her through. To get her revenge on the ones she had left behind.

She sat in her cave day after day, planning her sweet revenge.

Karma was all she could think about, until one day many years had passed and the other mermaids had forgotten all about her. They'd forgotten all about that fateful day and forgotten the sea witch existed.

So she was sitting alone in her anger, not realising that it was choking her. She had been forgotten and left alone and nobody cared anymore, the ocean had moved on outside her cave... and the only one she was hurting was herself.

All the sea witch had to do was swim out of her cave and look up. Up, up, up. Towards the blue sky above - and *swim, swim, swim.*

Then maybe she could be that little mermaid again.

Printed in Great Britain
by Amazon